CONVERSATIONS ON
CONTEMPORARY DRAMA

CONVERSATIONS ON CONTEMPORARY DRAMA

BY

CLAYTON HAMILTON

MEMBER OF THE NATIONAL INSTITUTE OF ARTS AND LETTERS

34288

A Series of Nine Lectures,
Delivered in Earl Hall, at Columbia University,
from February 11 to April 7, 1924.

New York
THE MACMILLAN COMPANY
1924

TO

THE THOUSANDS OF STUDENTS,

AT COLUMBIA AND ELSEWHERE,

WHO, FOR TWENTY YEARS, HAVE LISTENED

TO MY TALKS ABOUT THE DRAMA.

PREFACE

HERE is a book that was not written at a desk, but improvised upon a lecture-platform in the presence of an audience. It is a stenographic record of a series of informal lectures delivered in Earl Hall, at Columbia University, on nine successive Monday mornings, from February 11 to April 7, 1924.

When it was announced that this course would be open to the public, my friend Mr. George P. Brett, the President of The Macmillan Company, told me that he would like to publish the lectures in a volume. Mr. Brett had never heard me talk in public; and I perceived that he had assumed that I was a lecturer, of the sort that we so frequently import from London, who, appearing on the platform with a printed or typewritten pamphlet, proceeds to read it from the outset to the end, and, having done so, travels elsewhere, to read the same text to another audience. I hastened to explain that my public talks were not lectures in the formal sense, but merely conversations, that I carried nothing to the platform except the ideas in my head and the watch in my hand, that I improvised my conversations as I went along, and that whether I happened to be good or not depended mainly on the reaction of the audience. Since I did not plan my lectures in advance and rarely remembered an hour afterward anything that I had said, I could see no way to furnish Mr. Brett with the volume he was kind enough to wish to publish.

But Mr. Brett is a persistent gentleman, who is not accustomed to be thwarted in his purposes. He immediately offered to send a stenographer up to Earl Hall to take down every word that I said, and he suggested that, with a little editing, these stenographic reports could be prepared for publication. It was Mr. Brett's idea that, in this period of university extension, many people who might have liked to attend such a course of lectures if they had lived within commuting distance of Columbia University might like to have a record of the lectures made available to them in print.

I received this suggestion with considerable perturbation, because it seemed to controvert the only conscience that ever really troubles me,—the conscience of the craftsman. For twenty years I had practiced the two professions of lecturing and writing; but, in all that time, I had never written a single paragraph that I intended to speak nor dictated a single paragraph that I intended to print. I explained to Mr. Brett that writing was one thing and talking was another, that the technical processes of the two professions were entirely distinct, that my best writing would be unspeakable and my best talking would be unreadable; but he countered this argument with the suggestion that, if all my other books contained a record of my writing, there was no particular reason why this one book should not contain a record of my speaking.

After considerable hesitance, I agreed to try the plan as an experiment. I was afraid that I might suffer from stage-fright if I ever paused to realize that everything that I was saying was being taken down in shorthand and might subsequently be used against me; and it was, therefore, arranged that the stenographer should hide herself in the audience so that I should not see her and might forget that she was there. During the first lecture, I was a little worried and, every now and then, became too fussy with my phraseology for fear of the stenographer; but, after that, I actually managed to forget that the recording angel was present with poised pencil and to swing into my natural habit of talking to the audience without self-consciousness.

To read the stenographic records seemed as strange to me at first as the experience of hearing my own voice upon the phonograph or seeing my own figure on the motion picture screen. I had never known before exactly how I talked. I had always known that my manner of speaking was very different from my style of writing; for, in following the two professions, I had deliberately practiced different methods for the attainment of different ends. But I had never had an opportunity before to analyze exactly the various distinctions between the two technical methods of expression.

In writing for the printed page, the craftsman strives for literary finish, for finality of form; but this effect must be carefully avoided in talking to an audience. I have found in practice that the only expedient by which I can hold the attention of an audience for an hour is an appearance of unfettered spontaneity. This is the reason why I never plan a lecture in advance. I want, of course, to know enough about the subject to be able to talk about it at least five times as long as the lecture is to last; I want to know the leading points that I am likely to discuss, and the probable order in which I shall take them up; but I do not want to know beforehand the arrangement of details, and I try always to catch the mood which is to dominate the conversation from experimenting with the audience. My only notebook is the dial of my watch: as the minute hand goes round, I proportion my points accordingly.

The expression of the same idea is more compact in writing than in speaking. A thought which, on the printed page, would receive complete expression in one hundred words may require three or four hundred words for presentation on the lecture-platform. Because of the physical effort involved in listening, an audience cannot take in an idea that is expressed too briefly. For this reason, talk is necessarily thinner in its thought-content than writing. Repetition, which the writer especially avoids, must be practiced by the speaker as a technical expedient. He can see by looking at his auditors whether or not they have completely grasped the point he is expounding; and, if they have not grasped it, he must subtly manage to repeat himself without letting them perceive that he is doing so. Such a subterfuge is not necessary on the printed page. The writer may compact his thought into a single carefully written sentence; for this single sentence will stand there on the page, to be looked at whenever the reader may find it necessary to refer to it again.

The audience is an active collaborator in any lively lecture. A point that goes well with the audience will suggest others that are similar and will often tempt the speaker to digress from the main path of his discourse; and, on the other hand, an indication from the audience that the talk is growing dull may often require a sudden change of mood and an alteration of the plan of the attack. It is these acrobatics which are unforeseen that give a zest to lecturing and differentiate it from the more methodical and steadfast task of literary composition.

The writer, if his work is going badly, can lay his pen aside at any moment and try again another day; but the lecturer must keep on talking until his hour is up. Even when his thoughts come haltingly, he must never hesitate in his discourse; for, if he begins to fumble around for words, the auditors will be afflicted with that feeling of distress which arises from a subconscious desire to help him out. The speaker, therefore, must employ the readiest method of expression, even when he knows that it is not the best; he has no time to edit or rewrite a sentence in his mind while he is progressing from the initial capital to the terminal period. For this reason, the rhythm of speech is more brisk, more staccato, more headlong in its onward rush than the more deliberately modulated rhythm of written prose.

In preparing these stenographic records for the press, I have deleted a few digressions and cut out a few repetitions; but, in the main, I have left the text unaltered. I have made no attempt to rewrite it in literary terms. My other books were deliberately written to be read; but this book is frankly an experiment in the broadcasting of unpremeditated speech from the lecture-platform to a distant audience.

The name of the stenographer who took these lectures down is Miss Katherine King. I regret to say that I have never met her personally and should not recognize her if she should be sitting in the seat beside me the next time that I attend the theatre. But, whatever Mr. Brett may think of the result of our collaboration, it gives me a curious sensation to reflect that somewhere in the world there lives a lady whom I have never seen, but who nevertheless has written a book that bears my name upon the title page. I wonder how often she was bored when she was writing it, and how frequently she wished that I would think more keenly or express myself more clearly. Somehow I hope that she will never tell.

CLAYTON HAMILTON

NEW YORK CITY: 1924.

CONTENTS

CONVERSATIONS ON
CONTEMPORARY DRAMA

CONVERSATIONS ON CONTEMPORARY DRAMA

FIRST LECTURE

THE CONTEMPORARY DRAMA

FEBRUARY 11, 1924

ONLY a quarter of a century ago, when I was still an undergraduate in college, students were taught that there were three, or possibly four, great periods in the history of the drama,—the period of the Greeks at the time of Sophocles, the period of the Elizabethans at the time of Shakespeare, the period of the Spaniards at the time of Calderon (though our teachers were a little vague about this period, because few of them knew anything about it), and the period of the French at the time of Corneille, Racine, and Molière. At that time, toward the close of the eighteen-nineties, we were never told that the nineteenth century drama was worthy of studious consideration or that the contemporary drama was of any importance at all. Yet a great new drama had been launched into the world as long before as 1830, when the French romantics, led by Victor Hugo and Alexandre Dumas *père*, had revolutionized the art of the stage. This drama had been developed later by realistic writers like Emile Augier and Alexandre Dumas *fils,* and had been passed on to a great genius in Norway, the grim and tragic giant of the north. Henrik Ibsen had already attained his maturity and even passed the climax of his career in 1890; and his influence was making its impress in many other countries. A vivid new drama was launched in England by Sir Arthur Pinero in 1893 and was quickly developed by Mr. Henry Arthur Jones, Sir James Barrie, and Mr. Bernard Shaw. Germany came forward with the striking and infiuential plays of Hermann Sudermann and Gerhardt Hauptmann; the mysterious Maeterlinck appeared in Belgium; and important dramatic work was taken up and done in many other countries. Yet, when I was an undergraduate in college at the end of the eighteen-nineties, this contemporary drama was still considered unworthy of academic consideration, unworthy of serious study.

Of course, the only reason for so monstrous an anomaly was that the modern drama seemed too new and too near to our scholarly professors a quarter of a century ago. They were afraid it might not last, and they were not willing to run the risk of wasting any academic hours in a study of the possibly ephemeral. They did not know as much about the permanence of "Cyrano de Bergerac" in 1898, for instance, as we have learned in 1924. Time had taught them to be sure of Shakespeare; but they were not yet sure that Ibsen would outlast the nineteenth century. In this connection, I might remind you of an anecdote which some of you undoubtedly have heard. When Sir Arthur

Pinero, several years ago, was solemnly asked to formulate a definition of classic English comedy, he answered, "A classic English comedy is a successful farce by a writer who is dead."

I am very glad, however, that the academic attitude toward the contemporary drama has become more appreciative in the course of the last quarter of a century. Otherwise I should not be permitted to stand here, in a lecture hall of a great university, and talk to you, on nine successive Monday mornings, about plays that are actually being done in the theatre of to-day. But everybody nowadays—including even the most scholarly professors in our colleges—has at last become aware of the fact that we are living in the midst of a very wonderful period of dramatic creativity,—a period more vast and varied, more widespread and more versatile in its productiveness, than even those other great periods that I have mentioned,—the Greek, the Spanish, the Elizabethan, and the classic French. We are sure, at least, that the drama of the present period is great in quantity; and we have ample reason to believe that much of it is great in quality. At any rate, it is unquestionably worthy of serious study; and we enjoy the rare and great advantage of living in the midst of it and being able to watch it come into existence.

As students of the theatre, I think we should be rather proud of the fact that we are living in a period of such importance. A large number of centuries elapsed between the first two periods of greatness in the drama,—the period of Sophocles in the fifth century B.C. and the period of Shakespeare at the end of the sixteenth and the beginning of the seventeenth century A.D. Millions of people who were born and lived and died in that long interval of over two thousand years were not able to see any great play produced on a stage for the first time in the world. After the death of Molière, there was another interval of emptiness—not so long, indeed—a lapse of only one hundred and fifty to two hundred years—during which it was impossible for people anywhere to attend the first performance on the stage of any play of permanent importance. Yet, living in the present period, I have actually attended the world-première of several plays that seem destined to endure in the world's dramatic literature for centuries to come. In our own city of New York, which, since the war, has become the metropolis of the theatric world, we have frequent opportunities to observe the first production anywhere, or at least the first production in America, of plays that are immeasurably more important than any that were written in all the twenty centuries between Sophocles and Shakespeare. To remain obtuse to the contemporary drama, to refuse to regard it as worthy of most serious consideration, would be very much like living in Elizabethan London and neglecting to attend a performance of "Hamlet" or "Othello."

Yet the experience of living in a period of such dramatic productivity is so remarkable that it is a little difficult for us to appreciate the privilege. My own experience of theatre-going has covered a range of a third of a century. I began to attend the theatre regularly and systematically when I was about eight years old; and for nearly thirty-five years I have seen every play of any importance that has been produced in New York, not to mention plays that I have seen in other countries. That is not a long time, as history is measured: yet think how much has happened in those three decades and a half! When I began to go to the theatre, "Cyrano de Bergerac" had not been written. It is now established as an immortal masterpiece. When I began to go to the theatre, Sir James Barrie had not yet commenced to write plays. Mr. John Galsworthy had never been heard of; and I distinctly remember how queer I thought his name when I attended the first performance of his first play, "The Silver Box." Ibsen, of course, had nearly completed his life work when I was a boy, though I attended the first performances of his plays that were given in America; but think how much has been contributed to the drama of the world since the death of Ibsen! For instance, the entire literary movement that culminated in the establishment of the Irish National Theatre was launched less than thirty years ago; and it has given the world the deathless eloquence of J. M. Synge. Whenever we consider "The Playboy of the Western World," we feel as if it must always have belonged to dramatic literature; we feel, also, that the plays of Lord Dunsany must have existed for a long, long time; yet I was going to the theatre before these plays were written and, at the age of forty-two, I still persist in regarding my-self as a member of "the younger generation." All of you are so familiar with the plays of J. M. Barrie that I will wager that it is a little difficult for you to realize that your grandparents never had the opportunity to see them. "Peter Pan" is so familiar to us nowadays that it is hard to imagine a world in which this fairy-tale did not exist. Great plays are now so frequent that their occurrence has become almost commonplace. I dare say that that is the reason why we spend so much energy worrying over the decadence of the stage and wondering what we can do to reform the theatre. People are constantly writing to the papers, lamenting the low estate to which the drama has declined and regretting the good old days; and I suppose that people uttered similar complaints in the period of Shakespeare and the period of Sophocles.

One reason why it is difficult for us to realize the importance of the contemporary drama is that it has not as yet been adequately analyzed, adequately appreciated, and adequately celebrated by dramatic criticism. Of course, in the history of any art, creation always precedes criticism, since criticism is merely an analysis of what has been created. The critic cannot do his work until he has something to criticize. His function is not to tell the dramatist how to make great plays, but to tell the public how great plays have been made. Consequently, criticism usually lags a generation or so behind creation. The great Greek dramatic critic, Aristotle, was not a contemporary of Euripides and

Sophocles; he came a generation later, and saw their work in retrospect. It takes about that long for a great movement in art to find its great critic; and I dare say that it may be twenty-five or fifty years before the real significance of our present-day creation in the drama is adequately analyzed and definitely estimated by commensurate dramatic criticism.

In this country at the present time we seem to be unfortunately lacking in dramatic criticism. In saying that, I have no intention of disparaging the reviewing of current plays as it is handled so entertainingly and oftentimes so charmingly by the writers for our metropolitan newspapers. I think that the literary standard of our newspaper reviewing is unusually high; but I don't think that much of this reviewing has anything to do with criticism. What Aristotle was endeavoring to do was very different from what Mr. Broun or Mr. Woollcott succeed in doing so delightfully. I perceive that I ought to tell you what criticism is; but I haven't time for that—it would take at least an hour—and, besides, if you really want to know, all you have to do is to read Matthew Arnold. He will tell you, among other things, that the purpose of criticism is to see the object as in itself it really is,—to see *the object,* mind you, and to write about the object,—not to write about oneself. A theatrical reviewer may say, "I saw a certain play last night and I did not like it at all"; but this statement has nothing to do with criticism if the reviewer goes on to say that the reason why he did not like the play is that his little boy had kept him awake the night before with whooping-cough. When the modern English drama was initiated in the eighteen-nineties by Pinero and Jones, it was earnestly and seriously criticized by William Archer and Arthur Bingham Walkley and George Bernard Shaw; and the modern French drama has been excellently analyzed throughout the course of its development, because the French have a mind that is peculiarly adapted to the purposes of criticism. But dramatic criticism is sorely needed here and now, because the productive activity of the contemporary theatre is so vast as to be bewildering. There has never been a period in the past when there has been so much to appreciate, and so many different kinds of things to appreciate, in the drama of the moment; and it is difficult for the public, without critical guidance, to learn to appreciate at the same time so many different kinds of creative endeavor.

It is an important point that the present period is the first great period in history when the drama has existed as an international art, when the drama has been practiced in many different countries at the same time, and when there has been an active interchange of plays between the theatres of the different nations. This is the first time in the history of the drama when there has existed what I may call a standardized theatre,— that is to say, when playhouses closely resembling each other in their physical appointments have existed simultaneously in several different countries inhabited by different races speaking different languages. We take this as a matter of course; but, if we will exercise